GETTING TO KNOW THE WORLD'S GREATEST ARTISTS

TITIAN

WRITTEN AND ILLUSTRATED BY MIKE VENEZIA

CHILDREN'S PRESS®
A DIVISION OF SCHOLASTIC INC.
NEW YORK   TORONTO   LONDON   AUCKLAND   SYDNEY
MEXICO CITY   NEW DELHI   HONG KONG
DANBURY, CONNECTICUT

To Burt Joseph. Thanks for handling the tough part of publishing.

Cover: *The Emperor Charles V (1500-58) on Horseback in Muhlberg,* by Titian. 1548, oil on canvas, 332 x 279 cm. © Bridgeman Art Library International Ltd., London/New York, Museo del Prado, Madrid, Spain.

Colorist for illustrations: Dave Ludwig

Library of Congress Cataloging-in-Publication Data

Venezia, Mike.
  Titian / written and illustrated by Mike Venezia.
     p. cm. — (Getting to know the world's greatest artists)
Summary: An introduction to the life and work of the sixteenth-century
Italian artist Titian Vecellio, who is best known for his realistic oil
portraits.
  ISBN 0-516-22575-8 (lib. bdg.)   0-516-26975-5 (pbk.)
  1. Titian, ca. 1488-1576—Juvenile literature. 2.
Painters—Italy—Venice—Biography—Juvenile literature. [1. Titian, ca.
1488-1576. 2. Artists.] I. Title.
  ND623.T7 V46 2003
  759.5—dc21
                              2002005981

CHILDREN'S PRESS and associated logos are trademarks
and or registered trademarks of Grolier Publishing Co., Inc.
SCHOLASTIC and associated logos are trademarks and or
registered trademarks of Scholastic Inc.

1 2 3 4 5 6 7 8 9 10 R 12 11 10 09 08 07 06 05 04 03

Self-Portrait, by Titian.
c. 1576, oil on canvas,
86 x 65 cm. © Art Resource,
NY, Erich Lessing/Museo
del Prado, Madrid, Spain.

Tiziano Vecellio was born in Pieve di Cadore, a small mountain town in the north of Italy, around 1488. When he grew up, he became known as Titian, which was sort of a nickname. Titian spent most of his life in Venice, Italy. There he became one of the most important painters in the history of art.

The Pesaro Altarpiece, by Titian. 1519, oil on canvas, 488 x 270 cm. © Bridgeman Art Library International Ltd., London/New York, Scala/Santa Maria Gloriosa dei Frari, Venice, Italy.

Virgin of the Rabbit, by Titian. 1530, oil on canvas, 71 x 87 cm. © Art Resource, NY, Erich Lessing/Louvre, Paris, France.

Titian also became one of the wealthiest painters in the history of art. Families with lots of money and religious leaders were always asking Titian to create his beautiful scenes for their homes and churches.

Titian was always being asked to do his amazing portraits, too. Before Titian came along, no one had ever seen such realistic paintings. Titian could really make people look like themselves. He also let you know something about each person he painted.

For example, the man in the painting above looks like he's about to go out and do something important. He seems very smart as well as kind.

Eleven-year-old Ranuccio Farnese, shown below, was from a very privileged family. Even though Ranuccio is all dressed up in royal clothes and is holding a sword, Titian shows him looking a little worried. Maybe he's thinking about all the responsibilities he'll have when he grows up.

Ranuccio Farnese, by Titian. 1542, oil on canvas, 897 x 736 cm. © National Gallery of Art, Washington, D.C., Lee Ewing/ Samuel H. Kress Collection.

Titian also did lots of mythological scenes for dukes, princes, and kings. These are some of his most famous works. In these paintings, Titian showed gods and goddesses relaxing or enjoying themselves at parties.

He often used rich, creamy colors and exciting brush strokes to create a feeling of movement and fun. Unfortunately, these paintings are intended for adult viewers only. Kids may have to wait a few years to see them.

There's a story that when Titian was very little, he made colors from berry juice and flowers to paint a portrait of his father on the side of a house. Whether this story is true or not, it's clear that Titian's parents knew their young son had some artistic talent. When Titian was 10 years old, his parents sent him to Venice so he could learn to be an artist from the great masters there.

San Giorgio Maggiore, Venice, by Claude Monet. 1908, oil on canvas, 60 x 73 cm. © Bridgeman Art Library International Ltd., London/New York/Phillips, Fine Art Auctioneers, New York, USA/Private Collection/ © 2002 Artists Rights Society (ARS), New York/ADAGP, Paris.

Titian must have been amazed when he first saw Venice. It is one of the most beautiful and unusual cities in the world. It's built on little islands right in the sea. Instead of streets filled with horses and carts, Titian saw streets made of water!

Everyone got to where they were going by boat. Because of the reflecting water and mist, Venice often looks like a magical fairytale land. Buildings can appear pink, blue, yellow, or gold, and they sometimes seem to float above the water. For years, artists from all over the world have been inspired by this colorful city.

Grand Canal with Santa Maria della Salute, by Joseph Mallord William Turner. 1835, 36 x 48 1/8 in. © Bridgeman Art Library International Ltd., London/New York, Phillips, The International Fine Art Auctioneers, UK.

Detail from *Miracle of the Cross*, by Gentile Bellini. 1496-1497, oil on canvas.
© Art Resource, NY, Scala/Accademia, Venice, Italy.

Titian lived with his aunt and uncle in
Venice until he could find a master artist
willing to take him into his workshop.
Apprentices did hardly any artwork at all.
First they learned to mix paints, clean brushes,
and sweep up. Sometimes, they cooked for
other apprentices and assistant artists.
Anyone who wanted to be an artist in Venice
had to spend seven years as an apprentice.

Titian was lucky to enter the workshop of the Bellini brothers. Gentile and Giovanni Bellini were two of the greatest artists in Venice. Titian learned a lot from each master's style. By the time he was a teenager, Titian was allowed to paint small portions of Giovanni Bellini's paintings.

St. Francis in the Desert, by Giovanni Bellini. c. 1480, tempera and oil on poplar panel, 124.4 x 141.9 cm. © The Frick Collection, New York.

Titian also learned from other students in the Bellini brothers' workshop. One of his favorites was Giorgione of Castelfranco. Giorgione was 10 years older than Titian and was starting to do paintings on his own.

Titian loved the way Giorgione painted dreamy, peaceful scenes of people in beautiful landscapes. Giorgione knew how to use just the right touch of color, too. Titian was thrilled when Giorgione asked him to help paint a mural on the outside of a new building in Venice.

Sistine Chapel ceiling: The Prophet Ezekiel, by Michelangelo. 1510, fresco (post-restoration). © Bridgeman Art Library International Ltd., London/New York, Vatican Museums and galleries, Vatican City, Italy.

Aristotle and Plato (detail from *The School of Athens* in the Stanza della Segnatura), by Raphael. 1510-1511, fresco. © Bridgeman Art Library International Ltd., London/New York, Vatican Museums and galleries, Vatican City, Italy.

The mural Titian and Giorgione were working on was a type of painting called a fresco. A fresco is made by coating a wall with a thin layer of wet plaster. Then, watercolors are painted on the plaster before it dries.

Many artists of this time made fresco paintings, including Michelangelo and Raphael.

Those two famous Renaissance artists worked in the warmer, drier Italian cities of Florence and Rome. Even hundreds of years later, their frescos look almost new.

Venice, however, was so damp that frescos there didn't last very long at all. Today only small portions of Titian's fresco paintings are left.

Madonna and Child with Two Angels, by Titian. 1519, fresco, 160 x 350 cm. © Art Resource, NY, Cameraphoto/Palazzo Ducale, Uffici Direzione, Venice, Italy.

When Titian and Giorgione's mural was finished, almost everyone in Venice went to see it. People soon realized how talented these artists were. Titian started to get requests to do paintings all by himself. The painting above may be one of the first ones he did on his own.

Titian preferred to do most of his paintings with oil color on canvas. Oil painting was a fairly new discovery at the time. Venetian

artists knew oil paintings would last longer than frescos in their city's damp climate. It was much easier to move canvas paintings around, too.

What these artists really liked, though, was the richer, brighter colors they could get with oil paints. Artists could put their color on in thick globs or thin glazes. They were able to paint with moody, swirling brush strokes, something they were never able to do with watercolors.

The brush strokes in some of Titian's paintings are so beautiful and interesting, they seem almost like works of art all by themselves.

Detail from *Annunciation,* by Titian. c. 1564, oil on canvas, 403 x 235 cm.
© Art Resource, NY, Erich Lessing/Church San Salvatore, Venice, Italy.

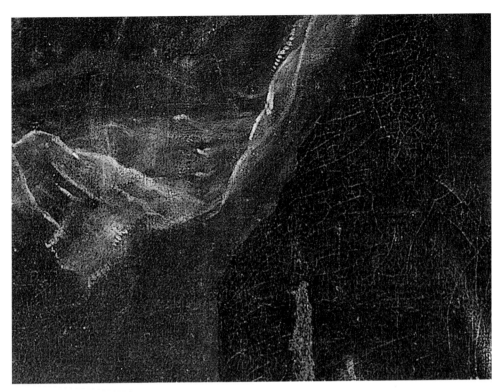

Detail from *Annunciation,* by Titian. c. 1564, oil on canvas, 403 x 235 cm. © Art Resource, NY, Erich Lessing/Church San Salvatore, Venice, Italy.

Detail from *Annunciation,* by Titian. c. 1564, oil on canvas, 403 x 235 cm. © Art Resource, NY, Erich Lessing/Church San Salvatore, Venice, Italy.

Titian was always trying new and different things with his paintings. Sometimes the people who paid him didn't care for his experimenting.

Titian painted the altarpiece shown on the next page for the Church of Santa Maria dei Frari. It's one of his most important and beautiful works. Church leaders were shocked when they first saw it, though. They thought the figures at the bottom were too large and would take attention away from the main figure of the Virgin Mary. They also thought Titian used too many bright colors, especially his favorite color, red.

Assumption of the Virgin, by Titian. c. 1518, oil on board, 690 x 360 cm.
© Art Resource, NY, Scala/Santa Maria Gloriosa dei Frari, Venice, Italy.

Assumption of the Virgin,
by Jacopo Palma (il Vecchio).
191 x 137 cm. © Bridgeman
Art Library International Ltd.,
London/New York,
Galleria dell Accademia, Venice.

But Titian knew exactly what he was doing. When you compare his painting to a similar one by Jacopo Palma il Vecchio, you can see how Titian filled his painting with more life, energy, and exciting color. Titian knew that when his painting was placed in the church, the color and the size of the figures would work just fine.

Photograph of the Church of Santa Maria dei Frari, Venice.
© Art Resource, NY, Erich Lessing.

The people of Venice agreed. They lined up for blocks to see this remarkable painting. They were proud to have it in their city.

Queen Isabella of Portugal, by Titian. 1548, oil on canvas,
117 x 93 cm. © Art Resource, NY, Scala/Museo del Prado,
Madrid, Spain.

Federigo Gonzaga, First Duke of Mantua, by Titian.
c. 1525, oil on panel, 125 x 99 cm. © Art Resource,
NY, Erich Lessing/Museo del Prado, Madrid, Spain.

Pope Paul III and Nephews, by Titian. 1545, oil on canvas.
© Bridgeman Art Library International Ltd., London/
New York, Museo e Gallerie di Capodimonte, Naples, Italy.

Suddenly, kings, queens, dukes, and religious leaders from all over Europe demanded that Titian do their portraits and decorative scenes for their palaces. Titian had so much work now that he had to hire assistants and train apprentices for his own workshop.

The Emperor Charles V (1500-58) on Horseback in Muhlberg, by Titian. 1548, oil on canvas, 332 x 279 cm.
© Bridgeman Art Library International Ltd., London/New York, Museo del Prado, Madrid, Spain.

Francesco Maria della Rovere, by Titian. 1536-38, oil on canvas, 143 x 100 cm. © Art Resource, NY, Erich Lessing/ Uffizi, Florence, Italy.

Portrait of Eleonora Gonzaga della Rovere, by Titian. 1537, oil on canvas, 114 x 103 cm. © Bridgeman Art Library International Ltd., London/New York, Galleria degli Uffizi, Florence, Italy.

Sometimes people had to wait months, or even years, to get a Titian painting. Kings, princes, and even the Pope often became angry with Titian for making them wait so long. When these important people finally got their lifelike, beautifully colored paintings, though, they all agreed the wait was well worthwhile.

Annunciation, by Titian. c. 1564, oil on canvas, 403 x 235 cm. © Art Resource, NY, Erich Lessing/Church San Salvatore, Venice, Italy.

As Titian got older, his style began to change. His colors became moodier and he used freer brush strokes. Titian also started using his fingers more and more to smooth and blend colors.

31

Self Portrait, by Titian. c. 1560, oil on canvas, 96 x 75 cm. © Bildarchiv Preussischer Kulturbesitz, Berlin/Staatliche Museen zu Berlin, Gemäldegalerie, photo by Jorg P. Anders.

Titian died in 1576. He lived to be somewhere around 90 years old. Many other great artists during Titian's lifetime created sculptures, architectural designs, and drawings, as well as paintings. Titian chose to spend his long life just perfecting the art of painting. That is why he is known today as the Prince of Painters.

Works of art in this book can be seen at the following places:
Church San Salvatore, Venice
The Frick Collection, New York
Galleria degli Uffizi, Florence
Galleria dell Accademia, Venice
Gemaeldegalerie, Vienna
Louvre, Paris
Museo del Prado, Madrid
Museo e Gallerie di Capodimonte, Naples
National Gallery, London
National Gallery of Art, Washington, D.C.
Palazzo Ducale, Uffici Direzione, Venice
Palazzo Pitti, Florence
Santa Maria Gloriosa dei Frari, Venice
Staatliche Museen zu Berlin, Gemäldegalerie, Berlin
Vatican Museums and galleries, Vatican City